Learning Organization Practices Profile

Michael J. O'Brien, Ed.D.

JOSSEY-BASS/PFEIFFER
A Wiley Company
www.pfeiffer.com

Published by

JOSSEY-BASS/PFEIFFER
A Wiley Company
989 Market Street
San Francisco, CA 94103-1741
415.433.1740; Fax 415.433.0499
800.274.4434; Fax 800.569.0443

www.pfeiffer.com

Jossey-Bass/Pfeiffer is a registered trademark of John Wiley & Sons, Inc.

ISBN: 0–88390-375-X

Printed in the United States of America

Printing 10 9 8 7 6 5

We at Jossey-Bass strive to use the most environmentally sensitive paper stocks available to us. Our publications are printed on acid-free recycled stock whenever possible, and our paper always meets or exceeds minimum GPO and EPA requirements.

Table of Contents

Introduction

A "learning organization" is an organization that has woven a continuous and enhanced capacity to learn, adapt, and change into the fabric of its character. It has values, policies, practices, programs, systems, and structures that support and accelerate organizational learning. Its learning results in changes in the ways in which individuals and the organization operate.

Organizational learning manifests itself not only in individual growth but also in team and system-wide development. Dialogue and discovery are the essential elements of a learning organization; they lead to a smarter organization that can respond to an increasingly competitive market.

The purpose of this profile is to enable you to take a diagnostic "snapshot" of your organization's learning capability. The picture that emerges should help your organization begin to explore how to improve organizational learning.

In this diagnostic questionnaire, you are asked to examine twelve subsystems in your organization that have an impact on organizational learning. Although it can be examined separately for convenience, a subsystem is a component that is not a separate entity but is linked to all others that form the whole. Each subsystem impacts the others. For example, managerial practices affect climate; climate affects work practices. The subsystems that you will assess are:

A. Vision and Strategy

B. Executive Practices

C. Managerial Practices

D. Climate

E. Organizational and Job Structure

F. Information Flow

G. Individual and Team Practices

H. Work Processes

I. Performance Goals and Feedback

J. Training and Education

K. Rewards and Recognition

L. Individual and Team Development

Within each subsystem, you will consider a number of policies, principles, and practices that form the culture of your organization. You will assess the extent to which your culture supports continuous learning and quality improvement.

Instructions for Completing the Profile

Completing this questionnaire is simple. Each item will ask you to consider the truthfulness of the statement for your organization, on a scale from 1 to 6, with 1 meaning "strongly disagree" and 6 meaning "strongly agree." Simply circle the number corresponding to your opinion.

The most important thing is to be honest, to state your opinion so that your organization truly knows what its people believe. If you find an item difficult to answer, please do not skip it; rather, circle the number that best represents your "gut response."

Items in section B ask you to rate the practices of executives. Executives are defined as those who have responsibility for the overall performance of the organization or a large operating unit. Executives usually report to the chief executive officer and together they form the highest decision-making team of the organization.

Items in section C call for you to rate managers. For purposes of this questionnaire, managers are defined as people who are responsible for supervising and helping to manage the performance of other people.

Before you begin to respond to the items, mark the level of organization that you are considering in the box below.

I am responding to this profile in relation to (*mark one only*):

☐ the entire organization

☐ my operating/business unit

☐ my department

When you have completed the profile, follow the instructions at the end for scoring and returning the profile.

The Learning Organization Practices Profile

A. Vision and Strategy

In our organization...	Strongly Disagree	Disagree	Somewhat Disagree	Somewhat Agree	Agree	Strongly Agree
1. The vision and strategy are continually updated, based on changes in the business environment and customers' needs.	1	2	3	4	5	6
2. People take into account the organization's long-term goals and strategies as they plan and execute their work.	1	2	3	4	5	6
3. We discuss trends and forces that drive current and future changes in our marketplace and industry as a normal part of our work.	1	2	3	4	5	6
4. We have a vision of ourselves as an organization in which learning and purposeful change are expected.	1	2	3	4	5	6
5. People have a broad understanding of our organization's structure, processes, and systems and how they are interrelated.	1	2	3	4	5	6

B. Executive Practices

In our organization...	Strongly Disagree	Disagree	Somewhat Disagree	Somewhat Agree	Agree	Strongly Agree
6. We are inspired to follow our executives toward our organizational vision.	1	2	3	4	5	6
7. Executives visibly lead and facilitate problem-solving efforts or special projects.	1	2	3	4	5	6

	Strongly Disagree	Disagree	Somewhat Disagree	Somewhat Agree	Agree	Strongly Agree
8. Executives speak about the connections between continuous learning, continuous improvement, quality, and business results.	1	2	3	4	5	6
9. We believe that our executives are proud of us.	1	2	3	4	5	6
10. Executives hold managers accountable for supporting the development of their employees.	1	2	3	4	5	6

C. Managerial Practices

In our organization...

	Strongly Disagree	Disagree	Somewhat Disagree	Somewhat Agree	Agree	Strongly Agree
11. Managers encourage us to pursue personal development as part of our jobs and to learn by doing.	1	2	3	4	5	6
12. Managers help their people integrate what they have learned in development or training programs by discussing business applications.	1	2	3	4	5	6
13. Managers communicate effectively with their employees about the employees' developmental needs and progress.	1	2	3	4	5	6
14. Managers encourage people to contribute ideas for improvements through individual conversations and/or group meetings.	1	2	3	4	5	6
15. Managers admit their own mistakes.	1	2	3	4	5	6

D. Climate

In our organization...	Strongly Disagree	Disagree	Somewhat Disagree	Somewhat Agree	Agree	Strongly Agree
16. We are not afraid to share our opinions and speak our minds.	1	2	3	4	5	6
17. We have a healthy sense of "play" about our work; it's o.k. to enjoy our jobs.	1	2	3	4	5	6
18. We work hard to eliminate "we/they" mindsets; we cooperate and collaborate whenever possible.	1	2	3	4	5	6
19. We treat one another as adults—as people who can think for themselves and be responsible.	1	2	3	4	5	6
20. People are interested in and care about one another.	1	2	3	4	5	6

E. Organizational and Job Structure

In our organization...	Strongly Disagree	Disagree	Somewhat Disagree	Somewhat Agree	Agree	Strongly Agree
21. Job rotation, ad hoc assignments, and/or cross-training (for other jobs) are used to build work-force flexibility.	1	2	3	4	5	6
22. We utilize self-directed work teams that have responsibility for work processes from start to finish.	1	2	3	4	5	6
23. Our work spaces are designed to allow for easy and frequent communication among those who work together most often.	1	2	3	4	5	6
24. We routinely modify work processes in response to changing circumstances or priorities or to improve efficiency.	1	2	3	4	5	6
25. We are reducing the number of rules, policies, forms, and procedures, allowing more individual judgment.	1	2	3	4	5	6

F. Information Flow

In our organization...

	Strongly Disagree	Disagree	Somewhat Disagree	Somewhat Agree	Agree	Strongly Agree
26. We utilize advanced technology to improve the flow of information and to enhance our communication with one another (for example, satellite TV, computer networks, electronic mail, cellular phones, or pagers).	1	2	3	4	5	6
27. We communicate key business information to all employees through channels such as organizational newsletters, department meetings, and/or all-personnel meetings.	1	2	3	4	5	6
28. Those of us for whom it is appropriate have learned to use our computer system effectively.	1	2	3	4	5	6
29. All of our employees receive quality, productivity, cost, or sales data relevant to their jobs on a daily or weekly basis.	1	2	3	4	5	6
30. As our work groups or project teams solve business problems or create new approaches, we communicate our learnings and results throughout the organization (through things such as memos, presentations, E-mail, etc.).	1	2	3	4	5	6

G. Individual and Team Practices

In our organization...

	Strongly Disagree	Disagree	Somewhat Disagree	Somewhat Agree	Agree	Strongly Agree
31. Individuals and teams are encouraged to identify and solve problems in their work areas.	1	2	3	4	5	6
32. In conflict situations, blaming is minimized so that people can openly and honestly discuss the issues and work toward solutions.	1	2	3	4	5	6
33. People and groups are encouraged to analyze mistakes in order to learn how to do it better the next time.	1	2	3	4	5	6

Jossey-Bass/Pfeiffer

	Strongly Disagree	Disagree	Somewhat Disagree	Somewhat Agree	Agree	Strongly Agree
34. We routinely ask one another for feedback on our performance so that we can continually improve our work.	1	2	3	4	5	6
35. We share our expertise and learn from one another through informal conversations and "storytelling."	1	2	3	4	5	6

H. Work Processes

In our organization...

	Strongly Disagree	Disagree	Somewhat Disagree	Somewhat Agree	Agree	Strongly Agree
36. We routinely and purposefully use systematic problem-solving techniques for solving difficult problems.	1	2	3	4	5	6
37. We routinely experiment with new approaches to our work; we try out new ideas.	1	2	3	4	5	6
38. When a group learns or discovers new information that would be helpful to others, that information is quickly disseminated throughout the organization (for example, through presentations, memos, computer networks, etc.).	1	2	3	4	5	6
39. When we engage in problem solving, we consider the "ripple" effects that various solutions or actions may have throughout the organization.	1	2	3	4	5	6
40. We learn from the marketplace through studies of competitors and/or other industry leaders.	1	2	3	4	5	6

I. Performance Goals and Feedback

In our organization...

	Strongly Disagree	Disagree	Somewhat Disagree	Somewhat Agree	Agree	Strongly Agree
41. The satisfaction of our internal and external customers is considered in our performance reviews.	1	2	3	4	5	6

	Strongly Disagree	Disagree	Somewhat Disagree	Somewhat Agree	Agree	Strongly Agree
42. As appropriate, people periodically renegotiate their goals with their key customers, suppliers, and/or managers.	1	2	3	4	5	6
43. We routinely give our suppliers (internal and external) feedback on the quality of the products and services they deliver to us.	1	2	3	4	5	6
44. We set our individual-development goals during an annual goal-setting process, rather than during our performance appraisals.	1	2	3	4	5	6
45. Individuals' performance goals are clearly aligned with the organization's strategic goals.	1	2	3	4	5	6

J. Training and Education

In our organization...	Strongly Disagree	Disagree	Somewhat Disagree	Somewhat Agree	Agree	Strongly Agree
46. Educational programs include skill training on "learning how to learn" from one's own experience and from others.	1	2	3	4	5	6
47. Educational programs include skill training on becoming more creative problem solvers.	1	2	3	4	5	6
48. We have diagnostic tools for individual development and/or developmental-planning processes available for everyone.	1	2	3	4	5	6
49. We assign special work projects in which people are given the time and support to learn new skills and knowledge, as well as do the work.	1	2	3	4	5	6
50. Formal training programs provide us with tools, job aids, or processes that enhance on-the-job performance.	1	2	3	4	5	6

Jossey-Bass/Pfeiffer

K. Rewards and Recognition

In our organization...	Strongly Disagree	Disagree	Somewhat Disagree	Somewhat Agree	Agree	Strongly Agree
51. People are recognized for being courageous, that is, for experimenting and taking appropriate chances.	1	2	3	4	5	6
52. Managers are rewarded for supporting the development of their employees.	1	2	3	4	5	6
53. We share directly in the profits of the business through a profit-based reward system.	1	2	3	4	5	6
54. We are not punished for making honest mistakes, for having tried something worthwhile and failed.	1	2	3	4	5	6
55. We are recognized for solving business problems or successfully meeting challenges.	1	2	3	4	5	6

L. Individual and Team Development

In our organization...	Strongly Disagree	Disagree	Somewhat Disagree	Somewhat Agree	Agree	Strongly Agree
56. Much of our ongoing learning comes directly out of our work experiences rather than through formal training programs.	1	2	3	4	5	6
57. Teams are given appropriate assistance with their development (e.g., process facilitation, team-building support).	1	2	3	4	5	6
58. People have individual-development plans that impact their performance in a positive way.	1	2	3	4	5	6
59. Work teams and long-term project teams have specific learning agendas.	1	2	3	4	5	6
60. Taking responsibility for our own learning and development is considered part of our jobs.	1	2	3	4	5	6

Instructions for Scoring the Profile

When you have completed the *Learning Organization Practices Profile,* tear out the Individual Scoring Sheet on the next page and transfer your scores as follows:

1. Column 1, Profile Items and Subsystems, contains spaces to write the numbers you circled for all items. Transfer the number you circled for each item on the profile to its corresponding space in this column.

2. For each subsystem, add up the scores you gave all five items and write that total in the space provided in Column 2, Raw Subsystem Score.

3. For each subsystem, divide the Raw Subsystem Score by five and write the resulting number in Column 3, Final Subsystem Score.

4. To help us build a data base, please answer the "other information" and "demographic" questions on the back of the Individual Scoring Sheet.

5. Return your Individual Scoring Sheet according to the instructions given to you when you received the profile.

Individual Scoring Sheet

1. Profile Items and Subsystems	2. Raw Subsystem Score	3. Final Subsystem Score
A. Vision and Strategy: 1.____ 2.____ 3.____ 4.____ 5.____		
B. Executive Practices: 6.____ 7.____ 8.____ 9.____ 10.____		
C. Managerial Practices: 11.____ 12.____ 13.____ 14.____ 15.____		
D. Climate: 16.____ 17.____ 18.____ 19.____ 20.____		
E. Organizational and Job Structure: 21.____ 22.____ 23.____ 24.____ 25.____		
F. Information Flow: 26.____ 27.____ 28.____ 29.____ 30.____		
G. Individual and Team Practices: 31.____ 32.____ 33.____ 34.____ 35.____		
II. Work Processes: 36.____ 37.____ 38.____ 39.____ 40.____		
I. Performance Goals and Feedback: 41.____ 42.____ 43.____ 44.____ 45.____		
J. Training and Education: 46.____ 47.____ 48.____ 49.____ 50.____		
K. Rewards and Recognition: 51.____ 52.____ 53.____ 54.____ 55.____		
L. Individual and Team Development: 56.____ 57.____ 58.____ 59.____ 60.____		

Other Information

61. What other issues, related to organizational learning, should this profile have asked about?

_____

_____

_____

_____

62. Do you believe that the organization will treat the results of this profile seriously and will use the data to improve organizational learning?

_____

63. What else would you like the organization to know that is related to this topic?

_____

_____

_____

_____

Demographic Information

Please provide the following information for demographic purposes. All data will be held in strictest confidence. Individuals will not be identified with the results.

Operating/Business Unit _____

Department _____

Job Title _____

Years in Current Job _____ Years in Company _____

Age _____ Gender _____

Today's Date _____

Thank you for your participation in this survey. Please return this sheet according to the instructions you received with the profile.

7550